Luna Triste Press

LUNITABOOKS.COM

All characters in this book are

fictional composites.

They do not correspond to specific

children or incidents

ARTURO HERNANDEZ SAMETIER

THE GOOD LESSONS

A Teaching Life with Gangs, Delinquents & Troubled Teens

COVER ART: ESMERALDA PIZA

To

The Barrio Clanton & Primera Flats

students of El Santo Niño

&

The Salt River Pima-Maricopa Indian

Community

1

White T-shirt and baggy gray work pants. About two inches taller than five feet. His pants were slit at the ankle, and they made a tent over his black high tops. I sat next to him in the eighth-grade dean's office. The chairs were hard, of a dark wood, a train station feel to them. The thirteen-year-old next to me couldn't get comfortable in one. "So, what did you do?"

"Nothing. They want to kick me out." He was anxious.

"Is your mother coming?" No answer.

"It's messed up. The dean says he found a screwdriver in my locker. It's not mine."

"Where are they going to send you?"

"I don't know. Probably on the bus somewhere.

"You're gonna have to wake up early."

"I'm not gonna go. Fuck the school."

It was my first week as a runner for the junior high truancy office, and Mr. Scanlan asked if I would make an after-school visit to the boy's family.

That evening, I wrapped some wool around myself for the January chill and kicked over the engine on my sputtering Honda 450. The coat flapped at the ends, and a cold, night jasmine rushed through the helmet. I twisted the throttle and flew over Dodger Stadium, then downshifted into Chinatown and the sudden aroma of spicy noodles and chicken fried rice.

At Sunset and Alameda, the corner of Olvera Street, the best taquitos in the world sang in three inches of bubbling fat. I was feeling anxious bothering a family this late, so I stopped and stalled long enough to down four of them and lick the salty green tomatillo sauce off the paper plate.

I jumped back on the bike and a few blocks later came in for a landing on the wino end of Main Street. The sidewalks squirmed as ragged folks stuffed newspapers in their shirts for warmth, made cardboard beds, built bonfires, drank, slept, argued and laughed. I cut my engine and backed up with my feet. Straight ahead, right across the street, a heavy woman in canary yellow hot pants sat comfortably on a fire hydrant. She was hollering and waving at traffic, grabbing guys by the elbow as they passed, calling them "honey."

I was parked in front of a tattoo shop, the owner standing on the sidewalk, his inked arms crossed.

"Don't see that every day. Or do you?" I asked.

He took a few seconds to answer, his attention on the show across the street. "Some guys will pay fifteen dollars for a woman like that."

Maybe he was one of those guys, so I shut up. I walked to the corner and entered the same brick building Mr. Scanlan had visited twice in the last week.

Except for the Alexandria Hotel—big and decent with a club on the first floor full of men wearing boots and ranchero hats—the hotels on skid row, with their faded tattoos announcing, "Modern singles, fireproof and furnished," were built decades ago for rail workers and the men who unloaded fish, vegetables, furniture and live pigs. Mexican families now lived in these hotels, and they had children who needed to be in school.

I followed directions under a yellow light that sent me to the end of the hallway.

There, I ran into a young man in his wire cage. A sign said his purpose was to keep out transients and rent out rooms. He was reading a magazine and *CHiPs* had an episode running on his five-inch TV. A tiny Erik Estrada was biking across the screen as I passed. I found my address on the second floor.

The boy I'd met that morning opened the door, and his amaretto complexion turned reddish as he stared back at me. He was dressed for an evening out: tan khakis and a Pendleton wool shirt starched and buttoned to the collar; a black hairnet whose seams formed a spider at mid-forehead; his pointy black Imperials polished to a shine.

"You look good, Gustavo. I like those Imperials. I'm here to see your parents."

He wasn't as friendly, or scared, as he had been earlier. I noticed for the first time that "Silent" had been tattooed between thumb and forefinger. I tried that.

"Silent, can I talk to your mom? We have to see about a new school."

He looked back at a woman walking toward the door and muttered, "*Leva*," a vague threat, as he circled around me and started down the hall.

"Buenas tardes, Señora. I'm the assistant to the truancy counselor. I think I just angered your son."

"I'm sorry. Don't pay attention to him. Is he in trouble again?"

She opened the door a bit wider. "Pasele Señor," and she asked me to come in.

"We're about to have some tacos. Can I offer you a plate?"

"If it isn't too much trouble."

We sat at a formica table, and she served on two white plates with intricate blue trim.

"Gracias, señora. I just started this job, and I was nervous about bothering you at night. But there are so many parents we can't find during the day."

"Esta bien," she answered. "I'm embarrassed that you have to do this."

"Quien es, mija?" came a man's voice from the living room. "Who is it?"

"He's from the boy's school," she answered.

A tall, older man with deep lines in his face, a white t-shirt and black work pants came into the kitchen. I stood up to meet the father of the house.

"I thought the boys were here," he said to his wife.

"Gustavo left when he saw the man at the door. I don't know where Alfredo went."

The dad sat down. His wife made a plate for him and brought a can of Pepsi with a dish of yellow peppers from the refrigerator. Neither seemed uncomfortable nor impressed by my presence. I let them know why I was there.

"Gustavo was caught with a screwdriver. He was already in trouble for fights and ditching, so they're going to send him to another school. The only one that will take him is in Van Nuys, and he'll have to go on our bus."

The parents looked at each other and then back at me, obviously perplexed.

"If he doesn't go now, how . . ." The mother paused and went to a different thought. "Since he started hanging out with the cholitos, he can't go anywhere without trouble. He'll be afraid."

"That's a problem, I know."

Neither one replied.

"Can I be honest with you?" asked the mother. "With my older son, Alfredo, I still have hope. Gustavo, I wish someone could take him away to a military academy. I sleep better when the police have him detained."

"I can tell that Gustavo can be stubborn."

I slipped my arms out of my coat to lay it back over the chair. It didn't feel professional, but the kitchen was getting warm.

"Alfredo is more noble," the father added. "But he gets influenced by his younger brother. He also doesn't go to school, but he's a good artist. My wife's father gave us the money to open a t-shirt printing store. Alfredo works there."

"Is he doing okay?"

"Yes," said his mother. "But another man from the school came and told us we'll be in trouble because he's working. "

She looked at my suspended taco and wiggled a finger that I finish. I took a last bite.

"Maybe I can talk to somebody. Sometimes there are ways to do things."

"Por favor, if you can do anything, because at the shop I watch him. And he works hard. If I send him to school, no one will watch, and he'll just go to the streets."

"And Silent?"

The father looked straight at me. "He told you to call him that?"

"At the door, when he was on his way out, I noticed the tattoo. He wouldn't answer to Gustavo."

"These boys have no respect for themselves or anyone."

The mother was sitting to my right, attentive and swallowing small bites of her taco.

"What gang is he with?" I asked. "I saw the tattoos on his neck."

Gustavo's mother didn't hesitate.

"Both my sons are cholitos, but Gustavo is the worst. Alfredo goes to the parties on the weekends, but he comes to work. And he does respect me. Gustavo, I have no control over.

"Since when?"

"Even as a baby he was difficult. When we came to Los Angeles, we had to leave him with my sister in Sonoita. I don't know how much that had to do with it, but he has always been angry, stubborn. They've kicked him out of every school he's gone to."

"I should have let you take him to Mexico," the father said. "My wife wanted to return with the children and live with her parents, but I wanted her here with me. I had no idea what was coming. I'm sorry now."

"Does Gustavo also work at the t-shirt store?"

"I don't like him there," she answered, her eyes wandering off for a moment. "He takes the paints and uses them to drug himself. I don't have an answer anymore."

"This is hard," I said, and took in a slow, audible breath. "Let me talk to my boss about Gustavo. Mr. Scanlan is a very kind, older man. I think he used to be a priest. I know you are ready to give up, but sometimes a new person can reach a teenager."

The father looked at me with little hope. "*Vamos a ver.*" We'll see.

"Is there a time when Gustavo is here, that I can talk to him?"

The mother gave me a small head motion for no.

"They go to a house full of gang members over by the school. The boys call it 'The Mansion.' I don't know why the police don't close that place or burn it down. I don't know who owns it, but they sleep there; and from what I hear, do whatever they want. My husband has tried to follow the boys, we've called the police but . . ."

Her hands lifted slightly off the table as she failed to finish.

"I think if I ask around, I can find that house. The kids at the school will know about it, and the police listen to us."

I wanted to leave them with something concrete, and that would make me feel productive. "I can help with that house. As for Alfredo, honestly, the people at the school can barely manage the kids that show up. My boss has a long list of kids to find, and we only get to a few. Nothing will happen if he keeps working."

"We understand," said the father.

I put on my coat and stood up. "It's a rough street outside."

"It's not bad," the father said. "The drunks don't hurt anyone, and you don't hear gunshots like you do in other parts of the city. We know the owner of these apartments, so the rent is very low."

The father walked me to the door, "We can save money in this country—something impossible where we came from. But we paid another price."

The next morning, I told Mr. Scanlan about the meeting, and he called the mother at the t-shirt store. He told her that if she would bring Gustavo, we would follow the bus and stay at the new school for the day. If he met with confrontation, we would try somewhere else.

Gustavo showed up. He and his mother were at the bus stop by six-thirty. Mr. Scanlan gave me a ride, and we followed the bus to Van Nuys. We parked in the school lot and walked over to meet him, but Gustavo wasn't at the bus as agreed. We looked over the various streams of students approaching the junior high and Scanlan saw him first.

"He's leaving. That's him walking toward the corner."

"Good eyes."

"Experience. To find this kind of kid, just look for the one who's doing the opposite."

We got back in the car and were following a little behind him when Gustavo paused at the corner. A car full of teenagers had stopped in front of him. Gustavo raised his t-shirt and stuck out his belly, with a huge "White Front" tattoo across it. We could hear words being exchanged while the t-shirt stayed up, and Mr. Scanlan gave me the radio to call security.

I froze as the boys in the car took aim with firearms Gustavo knew they would have.

2

My father was making his usual breakfast of chicharones, fried tortillas, refried beans, and a special chili made from the leftover fat ladled over the whole thing.

"They're out of control," he told me. "The Avenues are finishing off the boys from Highland Park. Yesterday they killed Huero."

I remembered Huero from an incident years ago. A cholo had been shot at the sidewalk entrance to my parents' business, the Monte Vista Laundromat. He was soaked in a blood pool and a crowd was gathering, waiting for the police. Seven-year-old Huero broke through on his bicycle and dragged the dying boy's blood into the laundry and round the new GE washers.

Now fourteen, Huero had become a regular petty thief. He would go to local stores and pilfer items. He sold them from a bicycle he rode with a metal leg, made necessary by a passing shotgun.

"All homeboys been shot in the leg. Bullets go down, that's why we run," he explained to my father.

Huero was frequently stopped by local police and would disappear for months at a time.

Yesterday, Huero was walking along Monte Vista Street when the carload of "Avenues" drove toward him. Huero yelled into the massive, five story Monte Vista Arms, hoping the Highland Park boys would respond. Huero often said that if the

Russians ever tried to take Highland Park, they'd be stopped at the Arms. "We have bullets up there. A lotta bullets."

But his friends were all on the roof, where many of them slept. When none responded, Huero reflexively exchanged gang signs with the boys in the car; and when a gun appeared out a rear window, he hopped toward my parents' Laundromat. The Avenues drove through the alley and caught him in the parking lot, carved him up, and draped him over the fence. It all took very little time.

"What else did you expect?" my father asked his mother as she stood there stunned. His cynicism came from a time when Huero was ten. The boy had written all over the Laundromat and then confessed when caught with markers. The mother had immediately argued, "How do you know it was my son?"

"Señora, the boy admitted it. It's good that he be honest."

She looked at her son and barked, "Why are you telling people that you do these things?"

Since then, my father had blamed her for the boy's troubles. But his judgment wasn't entirely fair. Her boys were hard to keep up with, and she spent too much time apologizing for them. Sometimes she just tired of it. She spent most of her days chasing them around, listening to angry teachers, neighbors and probation officers.

They had a younger son whom we thought might have a chance. The whole neighborhood remembered him as the boy who sat on the corner with his father, the tamale vendor. The boy was cute and would quote Bible verses to customers. But Sparky got a pipe to his head at three in the morning last year. And now Huerito was gone too.

After breakfast, I met my father at the laundromat. I helped him make another little cross out of wire and old machine parts. He walked outside and tied the metal cross to the long water pipe that ran the length of his laundry. My father put the new cross next to the one still there for Sparky. There was a cross for every boy killed in our alley. People occasionally put flowers on them.

3

Shorty was shy, soft voiced, adrift, schooled but without effect. A brown, moon-faced boy with doe like eyes. Shorty hadn't passed a class his whole ninth-grade year, but he was too old to stay back. I doubted he would attend high school.

I was sure Shorty could handle a job. He was honest. A gang member for lack of anywhere else to be. I met him not long after Gustavo was killed and took him under my wing. I let him hang out in the truancy office, and took him on a couple outings with my other drifters.

"Arturo's children," as the Jamaican secretary in our office called them.

I also met Nemo, Shorty's older brother, on a Friday when he came by the school in a white, early sixties pickup. Nemo was a hefty boy with cropped hair and deliberate speech. He didn't exert too much energy, but he was willing to talk.

"Nice truck. What year?" I asked, leaning into the passenger window.

"1962 Chevy."

"Going to fix it up?"

"I'm going to lower it and put on some rims. I got a shotgun hidden under my seat, so no one fucks with it."

"You just waiting for the money?"

"I got the money. Shorty doesn't need a job, he could work for me, but he's stupid. It's that *ruca*, his new girlfriend, that's bumping his head. I got his little sisters making more money." He paused to look over at his little brother. "Just fucking with you, Shorty."

"What do your sisters do?" I asked.

"Is this guy a narc or something?" Nemo's tone didn't seem worried.

Ignoring Nemo, Shorty said, "They take his stuff around to people, or people come around to them while they're playing. They're just nine."

"Cops are stupid," Nemo added. "They're always pulling me over thinking I'm gonna have shit on me."

They left for home in the truck. Just a couple of hours later, I was watching the KTLA evening news. There had been a killing at the L.A. Street Scene, the big festival on Broadway. I recognized the white truck.

Shorty showed up in the truancy office on Monday morning. He was seated by my desk when I walked in. I sank into my chair and turned to him.

"Was that Nemo?"

"You heard what happened?" he said, his body still and big eyes pointed at me.

"I'm sorry. I know he was a rough guy, but he took care of you. Good brother."

"He was parked at the L.A. Street Scene, and some guy came up to his window and fired. I called my mom, and she says they can't show his body cause his face is all messed up."

"Have you seen your mother?"

"No, not yet."

"We were going job hunting tomorrow, but we can go see your mom instead."

"Can we do both. I told Nikki about the job."

I picked him up the next morning where his girlfriend Nikki was staying. He had moved in with her two months previous, after the doctor said she was pregnant. Another reason he wouldn't finish school.

Lynwood, where Nikki lived, was once a suburb that called itself "America's town." After the Watts riots, real estate agents canvassed the area, "block busting," to get people to sell by saying that "Negroes from the riots are taking over." They spread rumors that resulted in quick commissions and cheap deals for clients who wanted income property. Renters replaced homeowners, dairy farms sold their small fields to developers, and the rural feel of Lynwood disappeared along with its spotted cows. Imperial Highway became cluttered with cheap motels catering to hookers. It was now a street that made you nervous at red lights and stop signs.

Shorty and his girlfriend were living in one of these motels. It was evenly brown, carpet to curtains. There was no air conditioning and the heat kept the toddler in a constant rash. The crying had them both sleepless.

On the slow ride from the motel to his mother's house, he told me how he had recently seen the president.

"We were in Beverly Hills knocking over parking meters."

"And you saw the president?"

"There were all these people at the end of the street, so I went to check it out, and the president was driving by in a limo."

"Shorty, you were robbing meters? With police everywhere?" I turned to see his expression. I didn't know people robbed the meters, much less in Beverly Hills.

"They were busy. We do it fast."

"How much did you make?"

"About two-hundred but we had to split it with everybody. I got thirty for the baby."

We got off at Macy Street, by all the big junk yards. We drove past Union Station and Olvera Street, where Macy became Sunset Boulevard. The Music Center was showing something new at the

Ahmanson, and the orchestra members were carrying odd shaped cases from the parking lot.

I parked in Silverlake and walked Shorty to the two-story apartment building where his mother rented. We heard a loud "Who is it?" and Shorty answered before opening the door.

His mother walked out of her bathroom and met us in the living room. She was a thirty-six-year-old with a thin figure and bleached streaks in her brown hair. She had a teenage quality about her, dressed in cords, Hush Puppies and a t-shirt.

"I'm sorry about Nemo. I met him just the other day. He was giving Shorty a ride from school."

"Nemo was my man. He took care of us. Every day this week, the devil's been after me. He waits under my bed and shakes it, but I know Jesus will protect me. This morning, the devil was shaking my bed, and I thought the babies could hear him, and I screamed, 'Jesus is with me!' That made him stop."

She stopped and asked us to sit down. I joined Shorty on the couch. His mom was still standing, cinching her robe to free up both hands.

"Shorty knows I'm not afraid. And I'm not one of those moms that's old-fashioned. They don't got anything they can pull on me," she said, her voice agitated.

"Why don't you help Shorty out. I've got my hands full, and I know something's in my head since they killed Nemo. I just want to find the fuck that did this and make him feel what I feel."

Back on the street, I asked Shorty about his dad.

"He died from a motorcycle accident. He and my mom used to ride together, but then he got hit and kept getting sick. That's when Nemo started dealing."

I bought Shorty a shirt at the Lynwood thrift and a twenty-five-dollar suit that fit like Charlie Chaplin in *The Little Tramp*. I had a letter on school stationery explaining that Shorty was a good kid in a special program and that we would appreciate an employer giving him a chance. An Asian man at the Lakewood Mall read the letter and said he would work something out. He taught Shorty how to stock and sell shoes, and he paid him a few dollars under the table. But the store owner didn't have enough work—he was just trying to help. By the end of the week, Shorty wanted to try somewhere else.

We decided to apply at the Arby's in the same mall parking lot. The owner, an older, tall and lean white-haired man, looked at the letter and asked us to wait. He came back in a few minutes with a tray of change and asked if Shorty was ready to interview. I turned to him, and Shorty nodded yes. The owner reached into the tray for a dollar bill.

"Let's say a Coke costs sixty-eight cents, and the customer gives you this dollar." The owner pushed the tray closer to Shorty.

"Go ahead Robert. Count the change back to me."

Nothing. Shorty's eyes just froze. He couldn't do it on paper either. He just had no idea.

"Look, I want to help you, Robert, but I can't have you at the register if you can't make change, and all our employees work all the stations. You have to cook, make change, take orders and clean."

"What if I can teach him?" I offered. "Can he come back?"

"If he can learn this, I'd be willing to give him a chance."

We worked on it for a week, counting money forward and backward. He picked up the idea at the end of the first day, and by the week's end he was getting confident.

We went back, and the man stuck to his word and hired Shorty.

But he only lasted five weeks because he had difficulty being on time. He wasn't used to it, the baby kept him up at night, the buses were slow to come again when he missed. On the bus, he was often hassled by other gang members because of the tattoo under his eye, his hair cut, clothing and mannerisms.

"Can't I go back to school?" he asked. "I feel like that's what I should be doing."

"Where would you live? And how about Nikki?"

I felt conflicted about my response. Father Sharp at St. Vincent's, who baptized Nikki's baby, had already warned me not to encourage Shorty and Nikki to get married. "Don't pile another problem on these kids."

It wasn't so much that I wanted them to get married, or Shorty on the career track at Arby's, but resources had thinned out at my end, and I just wanted him established somewhere.

"Maybe I can go home, and she can live with her mom again. I don't know, but I'm going to get fired and I keep thinking about school."

"You've got to decide something," I said. "Maybe you can go to the Job Corps like your friend David. I'm getting busy, and it's getting hard for me to take you around like this."

"I know you aren't always going to be here." There was no accusation in his tone.

He was right. We lost touch a short time after that conversation. It was one of many lessons for me in the uselessness of being the Lone Ranger, Mr. Ghetto Warrior.

4

Mr. Scanlan, counselor for the truancy office, had once been a priest, lastly at Blessed Sacrament in Hollywood. He left after thirty years. He was kind, without intention of marrying, and respectful of the church. He had just bought a car with ten-thousand dollars cash. We rode around in it, and he did most of the talking. I did all the chasing and translating.

Kids liked getting chased. Mr. Scanlan would drive up next to them, open the door lock and let me go. I'd run through alleys, around comers, through auto repair yards, and then the kid would turnaround, slow up and wait to be caught. I'd have a sweaty eighth grader in a one-armed hug, and he'd be both laughing and acting mad.

"Let me go Hernandez, or I'm gonna sock you."

I never got socked. The boys knew I would never chase them again, and there would go the afternoon adventures. When you ditch school all the time, it gets boring by midday. A good chase when you're thirteen hits the spot.

It was Monday morning, and Mr. Scanlan and I had started our rounds in his new Buick.

"My friends think it was stupid to take all my savings and buy a car," he said. "Arturo, this is probably the last car I will ever own. I've never had payments, certainly not as a priest." He showed me a list of the homes we had to visit this morning.

"You have perfect handwriting," I noted.

"It was Catholic school. The nuns made us do circles and circles. They don't teach that anymore. I think it was valuable." He drove slowly, a grandfatherly, tall gentleman in a sensible car. The Buick gave a nice ride, and it gave us time to talk.

Our first visit that morning was to the north-east side of USC, on a street with student housing on one side and the ethnic swell on the other. That same week, two coeds had been attacked by fifteen-year-old boys, and the campus paper was advising women to stay on their side of the moat.

The Victorian homes in this area had been subdivided into rooming houses, so you never knew who would answer the hallway door. At our address, the girl we were sent to find answered the chime.

She hadn't been to school in several months.

Marisela let us in and pointed us to the couch. She brought a chair from the kitchen for herself and sat in front of us. She pulled down her knit blue miniskirt, which matched her halter and eye shadow. She was a pale, meaty girl with streaked blond hair. Her mother joined us on a dark green lounger. She was not old, but she was small, wrinkled, and tired.

Like moms we found everywhere—Van Nuys, Pico-Union, Hollywood, or the East Side—she seemed exhausted, without a clue why her children didn't do what others did, having little to offer except an apathetic politeness. She understood her daughter had been ditching, looked at her, looked at us, back at her.

I went through the usual questions, asking in Spanish, "And why haven't you been to school, Marisela?"

"I don't know. I don't like it. I'd rather work."

"What does your daughter do for work, Senora?"

"She helps a man sell jewelry."

I told Mr. Scanlan the girl was selling jewelry for a man instead of going to school. Scanlan told Marisela it was good that she worked, but she would have to come back to school. It was the law for a fourteen-year-old. We would expect her in the morning. I translated this to Marisela's mother.

Her perfunctory, "I understand," made me uneasy.

Mr. Scanlan saw that I appeared to be waiting for more in her reply. "Do you want to talk to her for a little while, Arturo?"

"I'd like to ask her if she wants Marisela to go to school. She doesn't really seem enthusiastic for the idea."

Scanlan made himself comfortable. I noticed a small tattoo peeking out of Marisela's shoe when she bounced her foot.

It spelled "HARPYS" in Old English lettering, the kind favored by gangs in this area.

The Harpys gang roamed a section of tenements to one side of USC, but its members lived tenuously between the monster 18th Street gang to the west and the older Clanton, Primera Flats, and Diamond Street gangs to the east.

I now had questions for both Marisela and her mother. "Senora, I sense that there might be a reason that Marisela is better off at work. I noticed the tattoo on her foot."

Her mother stared at me. She appeared to be organizing her thoughts, choosing words.

"She is not a bad girl, but she does nothing at school except get together with those cholitos. I gave her a choice, and she chose work. At least I know where she is all day. I can take her to your school every morning, but can you guarantee that someone will know where she is or that she won't leave? I know you can't. I also know that if she gets into any trouble, you're going to send her to schools far from here, and how will that help? I can barely keep my eye on her here. It doesn't make sense, does it?"

She looked at Mr. Scanlan for a moment and then back toward me. She still had a little more to say.

"If I'm going to spend my days going to meetings that don't result in anything, I might as well have her with me. If you can't offer some solution to this girl's problem, then let me handle it my way."

Her eyes were locked on me. I'm sure she had rehearsed this speech from the day she let Marisela stop attending.

I told Mr. Scanlan what Marisela's mother had said. His reply didn't soothe me, but it contained all the facts: "Arturo, the law states that she has to be in school. We'll try to get some help for her, but, no, we can't guarantee anything. Let her know we'll be back, and we'll put some thought into this. But we do expect her in the morning."

I translated this to Marisela's mother carefully and without threat. Mr. Scanlan then asked Marisela if she understood, and she answered a very polite, "Yes."

In the car, while Scanlan penned notes into his log, I said, "Marisela looks like a prostitute."

"No, more likely she's just growing up too fast. Her mother certainly wasn't swayed by us. I hope I didn't push too hard. We'll come back."

He was my boss, but I could talk with liberty. I shared what bothered me about the visit. "I don't know, Mr. Scanlan. I mean, honestly, can we offer anything better than what she's doing? She's already wearing a little gang tattoo."

"Not really, Arturo. Not at this point. We can work on it, but you know the district is cutting my hours. I'll have to work three schools instead of one next year. We can't tell people they can break the law, but we don't want to make a situation worse, either."

Scanlan turned his ignition and quietly rotated his new steering column. I looked across the street at the university apartments and wondered if the blond girls jumping out of their convertibles ever talked to Marisela. We came back a month later, but a different family answered the door, and then other kids took our attention.

5

Puppet claimed the local Primera Flats gang but met a boy from Diamond Street, so she spent a lot of time with him downtown, sleeping in cars, in parks, in different people's basements or their floors, and sometimes on the roof of the Mayflower Hotel, where Diamond Street *veteranos* often spent the night.

Her sister Heidi, a minute fourteen-year-old who went by Shy Girl, but wasn't, had been one of the rare success stories. I had surrounded her with college volunteers, girls who tutored her, took her to classes at USC, treated her to lunch and called her at home. Heidi's mother made a believable bluff of following her class to class unless she stopped ditching. For Shy Girl, it was enough at the right time. Some leadership emerged, and after she learned to play volleyball from one of the USC volunteers, she took herself to the park and asked if she could start a team.

Shy Girl asked me if I could also do something for Puppet, her sister. She had shrugged off my previous questions about her sibling, said they weren't close anymore, and that she had no idea about her. But Shy Girl had started to worry that her sister was in the kind of trouble you didn't come back from, especially as she heard rumors.

"She stays at that cholo house. That's what everyone says."

"The Mansion place?"

"It's not a mansion, Mister. We should go find her."

"Let me ask Mr. Scanlan and the assistant principal. I'll get you out of class after lunch. How far is it?"

"We can walk."

Crossing the school yard, I saw two boys fighting outside the truancy office. I tried to separate them, but one of the combatants accidently beaned me with a trash can when I grabbed his adversary. The Title 1 administrator, Mrs. Lewis, a large, grandmotherly woman, had no trouble settling things down. Juan, our custodian, pulled me back into the office and took the ice tray out of our mini fridge and snapped two ice cubes with a rap on my desk, poured them into a paper towel and handed me the bundle.

The bump made me a source of comedy in the office. Everybody had jokes.

I gave Shy Girl a pass to check out of fifth period and meet me in the assistant principal's office. Mrs. Nuremberg wanted to make sure I understood we were only to assure it existed, and to check if the student in question was staying there. We were not to enter if it looked dangerous.

Puppet would later describe to us what had occurred the night before we arrived:

She remembered putting on makeup—a thick white base and eyeliner to her ears, plucking her eyebrows to a thin line, and applying a heavy rouge with black lipstick. She took the bus to Maple Street and walked to the abandoned house where her friends hung out.

She had random memories of the next few hours: Big Sleepy, an older gang member who painted the butcher shop's mural, taking a hit of acid and getting frantic when his tiny white papers blew out over the sidewalk. Popeye and Droopy sniffing paint and Goofy, whom no one had ever seen sober, dazed from sniffing glue. Sharky showed her his sherm stick, a cigarette dipped in PCP, which he and Creeper were passing between them.

She saw Shotgun, a very tough girl dressed in black jeans and sweat top taking hits of acid on the front steps. Little Joe was drunk, and Mike, who lived in an abandoned car and everyone knew was crazy, was seizing after taking a deep inhale of Popeye's paint filled rag.

Little Joe tried to grope Shotgun, but even stoned, she fended him off. He then went downstairs where Puppet said she had fallen asleep on the couch. Dreamer admitted later that Little Joe was the one with the idea. He told Dreamer, "Puppet thinks you're cute. You go first. We'll put her on a train."

Because of the fire, the living room had fallen into the basement, and several feet of front wall had also disappeared. What remained on the sunken floor were a charred sofa, some chairs and a card table. Blankets, rags, bottles, cans and cigarette butts littered the space around the sofa. Puppet recalled a streetlamp and shadowy gray figures of gang members, with firefly points coming from their cigarettes. Art Laboe was playing oldies and taking dedications on KRLA.

Shy Girl and I walked up Figueroa a few blocks, twisting our way through a crowd of Vietnamese and Latina ladies exiting sewing shops and gathered around the lunch truck. We turned down Thirteenth Street toward Maple.

"She's in that house. That's the Mansion."

It was obvious the house had once risen handsomely, two stories with an attic. Burnt furniture sat on the yellowed grass, surrounded by paint cans, beer cans, shoes, bottles, bike parts and a TV. In the middle of the lawn rested an orange couch with a very sleepy boy on it. We came up over him, and his head popped up. His eyes were watery, and the whole lower half of his face was covered in silver paint. I recognized him.

"Grumpy," Shy Girl said, "Mr. Hernandez is here to talk to you."

"Who?"

"The counselor. Don't act stupid."

I needed to take charge of this situation.

"Heidi, I think we should look for your sister. This has to be fast."

Grumpy gave up trying to sit, and let his head fall back on the couch. "Homeboys bad a party last night."

We left him and walked around to the back of the house. The sumo figure of Little Joe and his round, shaved head moved toward us.

"Watchale," he said sarcastically. "Shy Girl brought a narc."

"That's Little Joe," she told me.

"Whasup, Homey," he said, round bodied like the Michelin Tire man. "You come to close down our canton? You missed out, Homeboy. We put Shy Girl's sister on the train last night."

I could see that Puppet was asleep in a huddle with two boys on the basement floor.

I recognized Sharky and Popeye from the junior high school. They wore extra-baggy pants that billowed at the knees. They practiced a walk where their knees almost touched the ground before bouncing up in the jerky, stylized gait of a marionette. You could see them coming.

Between them, they were carrying a truck fender across the lawn, still managing to bob as they walked.

"Insane, no brain!" Sharky yelled as they got closer. "How you like this poem Hernandez. 'When I was from Flats, I was bad, Now I'm from Clanton, I'm *maton*.' It's bad, huh Homie.

"Where's Mrs. Lewis," Popeye asked, his mouth still covered in the previous night's silver paint.

"About ready for school?" I asked.

"Yeah, Homeboy. Nah, I'm taking a vacation today, me and Sharky. Tell your Uncle Popeye what you want."

"Are you hiding the rest of the car in your pants?" I knew Popeye was fun to kid. Though this probably wasn't the time.

"Ooo, shit," someone said. "Homeboy's baggin' on your pants."

"Bet you could fit Little Joe on that forehead, Hernandez."

A diminutive African American girl in cornrows joined the conversation.

"You tell that big old white man I see you with to stay out of my business. I might shoot him with a bullet." The burned out, open kitchen was getting crowded.

"I'll tell him when I get back," I said. "What's your name?"

"You don' t need nobody's name. And you're just an assistant. What you doing here?"

Everyone started complaining.

"You can't arrest nobody,"

"Chale, take out the cuffs, Homes"

Sharkey came up to my face and faked a punch, slapping his fist into his palm.

"I'll have to knock you out, Homes."

Shy Girl didn't like this banter. "He only came to get Puppet."

"Shale, Droopy said to me. He had a lisp where he couldn't pronounce *Chale*. "You should have come last night."

Droopy and Popeye were standing next to each other, both still covered in paint, swaying and grinning.

"Heidi," I said, "do you want to try and get your sister?"

"You have to, mister. She's hardheaded."

The little girl in cornrows asked, "What you want with her?"

"I might have a job for her. And her mother is worried." I looked in Puppet's direction. "You know that's not right."

"No one forced her," Popeye said. "Why don't you give me a job?"

"Cause they don't got jobs sniffing paint," Little Joe informed him.

"Maybe they got a job being fat and stupid," Popeye shot back.

The cornrow girl moved in front of me, looking up from a few inches down. "Do we have to go to school to get the jobs?"

What I answered changed the rest of my life.

"No, you don't have to back. I know we can't make you. I'm tired of chasing all of you around. I'm going to open a school just for you guys. For Flats and Clanton. We'll get jobs and you'll like it there."

Everyone followed me down to where the living room furniture had fallen through to the basement. Shy Girl put a blanket from the floor over her sister. The boys next to Puppet woke up hard, and Puppet was obviously disoriented. There was no way to walk her back to the school.

I tapped Shy Girl's shoulder and nodded for her to follow me. The kids had made a stairway from crates, and we used it to get out of the basement and onto the lawn. "We'll get Mr. Scanlan and come back for her, with a car. She'll be sober by then."

Heidi and I walked back to the school. I had a feeling that social workers or the police would be needed, and I told Heidi I would be calling as soon as we arrived.

Shy Girl didn't argue. I saw the look on her face when she threw a blanket over her naked sister.

"Mister, you can't open a school. I know you were just talking." We had walked at a good pace and were just waiting for the last light to change. "That was dumb. You're going to get in trouble. For sure they'll ditch now."

6

Heidi was right. But when you don't know better, and you pursue something with joy and a sense of inevitability, grace and serendipity are predictable.

I told my administrators what I had said to the troubled bunch at "The Mansion." Instead of seeing it as a problem, or even asking why, Mr. Ikeda and Siskel said, "Look into it." I did. There was an empty warehouse behind the junior high school. Several meetings were held to explore the possibilities. The chief of police, city councilwoman and school superintendent showed up, and for a moment it was close to done.

A lot of haggling followed, but the estimates to purchase the building shot past the district's ability to pay. Students and parents had been following the effort through newsletters and rumor. Truant teens asked about the school when I picked them up, and I saw their excitement. There was no way to back down.

That June, I took a job a few blocks from the junior high. Catholic Charities operated El Santo Niño, a small community center that had summer employment. A very progressive order of nuns ran the place and soon my lost kids from the junior high were coming over for activities. Sister Natalia even hired Sharky, Smiley and Droopy to help with summer camp.

The auditorium was empty during the day and I began visualizing a one room schoolhouse, but I would need a salary as well as furniture, books and supplies. I was twenty years old and had no idea where to look for money.

Serendipity. Grace.

We had a soccer team funded by the Sugar Ray Youth Foundation. They provided equipment and a bus ride to games. I coached the team and decided to add a couple of the gang members. I still hadn't mailed in their insurance cards but took them to a game anyway.

They disappeared as we unloaded the bus, but were back at halftime with yard tools they had pilfered from the neighborhood. I got angry and told both they had to play. No leaving the area, and I put Grumpy on defense even though he was wearing tennis shoes. He slipped on the grass and broke an arm.

I received a call from the foundation saying that I needed to come to their office to discuss a bill they had received from General Hospital. I was nervous, wondering how responsible I would be for everything. I arrived and waited until a gentleman said they would see me now, and by the way, Sugar Ray was in the building and would be in our meeting.

Sugar Ray Robinson, the great retired champion, was still a formidable figure. He shook my hand and sat across a desk from me. Two other men joined us, and I began by apologizing.

He raised a hand for me to calm down.

"These things happen. I just need to hear the facts with these gentlemen. So, what exactly happened."

I explained.

"That was a mistake, son. Big one. Not because of the money, but you lost your cool."

Sugar Ray asked to see the bill and signed a check. He was going to shake my hand again when I said "Mr. Robinson, those kids I took. I promised to start a school for them. I have a building, but I don't have the money . . ." He stopped me.

"You're asking me for money."

I could feel the heat in my face. I'd been out of line.

"I know all about needing money. My foundation spends millions. Every year I go out to politicians and donors and do what you just did. They always start by saying, '*If* the budget passes, or *if* this or that committee approves,' and I stop them. No one uses 'If' with Sugar Ray Robinson. They learn to use 'how.' Not *if* but *how* are we getting this done. There is always a 'how' if you insist on finding it."

The boxer told me that if I could prove how a twenty-year-old would legally start a school, and if I could find one other person or group to believe and fund me, he would at least match them—with his own, not the foundation's money.

I called Sacramento and spoke with the office that regulated private schools. It turned out there was little. If the building met code and had two exits, and the teachers were over eighteen, the state would issue a legal permit to operate.

For the money, I spent weeks in the library and the phone book; I made calls and wrote letters. I had nothing to show for it. There were no grants for this kind of situation. Then my van was stolen from the community center, and I spent a few weeks back on the bus.

I lived at the beginning of the line, but within a mile there were people standing. There was no chivalry: young men like me sat comfortably while old ladies took flight in the aisles every time the bus came to a halt. They were too weak to hold onto the rails, and only the other bodies, thickly packed, kept them in place.

On the evening bus back to Highland Park, we picked up workers from the Farmer John plant, as well as people who worked for the produce wholesalers, the

Chinese fish market and the live poultry dealers. It was a whole different smell coming home.

On one such ride, a Vietnamese girl sat next to me. We rode a few more stops, and then an old blind man in a black sailor cap got on. He tried to find a clearing for himself as people did football maneuvers to get on or off. The girl stretched out her arm, grabbed the blind man's hand, and pulled him toward her. With one more move, she got up and pushed him into her seat.

Her consideration embarrassed me. I offered the Vietnamese girl my seat and stood in the crowd. With my arms stretched to hold onto the overhead rail, I busied myself scanning the small ads that formed a row over the windows. Sandwiched between ads for credit dentists and personal injury lawyers was something different: an open hand against a black background, with small white letters offering seed money for community self-help projects.

Sister Natalia wrote her recommendation and passed my proposal to Sister Cahill, the director of Catholic Charities, who gave it personally to the Campaign for Human Development. The awards committee asked her bluntly, "Do you really believe in this project?" She vouched for it, with little but her gut to go by.

Sugar Ray wrote another check, this time from his own account, and matched the ten thousand from the Campaign. I had an auditorium, a permit, and the money to run a school for two years.

El Santo Niño

Part 2

7

The neighbors called it, "*La Escuela de Los Cholitos*," the school of the little gang members. True, you couldn't get in unless you were a gang member, and except for Lala, who was from Diamond Street, and Lil Man, who was new in the neighborhood, the students had to be from Primera Flats or Clanton.

Sharky was thirteen and the youngest member of the class. Yogi, who would be twenty soon, was the class senior.

But that fact of gang membership wasn't the issue. They were a friendship group of kids in trouble, and each had his or her own reason for the trouble he or she was in. Similar kids in another cultural or economic group, or in a different geography, might not have been in a gang, but they would have self-mutilated, committed suicide, developed eating disorders, abused drugs, become depressed or run away from home.

The problem was never simply a drunken dad, a negligent mom, lack of an afterschool job, bad public schools or peer pressure. I knew their parents, and I knew their teachers. In this same neighborhood lived thousands of teenagers with similar backgrounds. The students in this auditorium had histories of trouble, both at home and in school, but the reasons varied from kid to kid.

Pirate carried with him a visible angst that made him partial to self-medicating. He had two hardworking parents who had always involved themselves in his schooling, taken him to Little League, and done all the right things. For his brothers and sisters, it had worked. But for Pirate, all six-foot-five of him, it just wasn't enough.

Creeper was never still. His body consisted of one thin bone, and he had a "lazy eye" on his left side. A hyper kid who was as squirmy and hard to pin as a fish. His grandfather, who was raising him, was trying, but it wasn't enough.

Smiley had a good heart and loved to dream, just like his brothers. But his mind had difficulty keeping things in order. At fifteen, he could not add simple numbers or name the planet he was on, even though he had a sister in college and successful, blue-collar parents.

Sharkey couldn't read. Not at all. He was not dumb, had eight years of schooling behind him, and yet he struggled to complete the alphabet and didn't know how to sound out syllables.

Playboy was smart, articulate and handsome. A standout among these boys. He enjoyed being a big fish in their small pond, was bored and needed to be reined in before he ruined a reachable future.

Happy moved through life daydreaming, drinking, and scared of the bullets that followed him as he rode his bike home. He was a good-hearted, big girth of a kid. His parents often came over and thanked me for working with him. "He's a good boy, just confused," they would tell me.

Sad Eyes and Lala were two bright girls bored with public school and attracted to gang boys. But they were not the type of girls to be victimized. They considered themselves cholas, but they had ambitions and didn't get mixed up with the drug culture beyond sharing a joint.

Psycho wasn't mean, but he was like a giant, muscle bound eight-year-old. Before he knew it, he was doing something stupid. He needed self-control and lots of it. He walked home without pants one day because Sad Eyes' brothers gave him a thrashing and stripped him naked. It was payback for what happened the previous day: Psycho impulsively pawed at and tried to grope Sad Eyes as she left class. He was sorry the minute after he did it, but too late to pacify her family.

Woody was a typical bad boy with poor academics, but he had a work ethic gained from helping with his father's janitorial business. A young man on the verge of insight and maturity, he just needed a bit of catching up, and like most teenagers, some mentoring from someone who wasn't his parent.

Droopy could fix television sets, had two siblings on the way to college, and made great company and conversation. But he had a fuse in one hand and a blow torch in the other. Once angry, nothing mattered, and only regrets followed. His addiction to paint made it worse. He was always good when he was with me or with a relative, but this couldn't be all the time. Regular public school, seated for an hour at a time, was impossible for him. The school district wouldn't take him back since he beat up a teacher. I rarely had problems with him, but I understood how he was geared, and I had the flexibility to shift demands.

Shadow, Sharky's older brother, was an example of the typical slow learner, the mildly retarded. He loved being in juvenile hall because prison life was predictable and the slow, structured classes worked for him. In jail school, everyone worked at their own pace. Outside of juvenile detention, he spent his days high on paint and quietly following the other boys.

At six-foot-four and over two-hundred pounds, Yogi moved like the big bear he resembled. He was never violent and not a drug user. All the boys liked him. He had dropped out of school in the seventh grade and was running an auto painting business from his parents' front yard. He belonged to the gang because they were the only kids around during the day.

Spanky frustrated teachers. He was a fourteen-year-old with the maturity of a seven-year-old. He was not dangerous, but lazy, a bit spoiled and childish. As a rule, he would stare at a teacher all year without ever putting a pencil to paper. He seldom passed a class.

Sparky, like Playboy, had smarts, never engaged in violence, and seldom went beyond moderation in drug use. He was a genuine businessman, and unlike the other gang members, he made serious money in the drug market. He knew how to save and was a busy guy. He didn't have time for shenanigans.

Casper's father pastored a small local church, but Casper suffered a heavy addiction to paint, sherm sticks and alcohol—though he was always helpful and polite. Like Happy, he had a fundamental intelligence that had never been tapped or acknowledged. In class, he required constant refocusing and reworking of school material into smaller chunks. If that didn't happen, he just sat wearing a passively vacant expression and retained nothing. He was a sweet boy, but he was very willing to get in your face if put down or threatened.

The school psychologist at Adams Junior High School had assessed Goofy as having an above-average IQ. He possessed a subtle sense of humor, but also a learning disability that prevented him from exercising his gifts. He spent his days, morning till evening, stoned at the park, staring at the sky and talking nonsense. Hence, the name Goofy.

Lil Man scowled all the time. He was a small, angry African American kid who wore a blue cap that shielded his eyes and squashed his curls. Completely illiterate, and scared of anyone finding out, he was a sweet, no-nonsense kid as long as he wasn't threatened.

Joker, like Yogi, limited his participation in the gang to partying and kicking around with some of the boys. Of noble character and not violent or criminal, he had an aging mother to take care of and had dropped out of school at a young age to work. His drug use never went beyond something remedied by menudo and Tabasco the next morning.

Peanut measured four-feet, ten-inches. She was a slight, pretty girl with long black hair who paid attention to nothing but boys. Most days, getting Peanut out of bed involved a protracted struggle between her and her mother. Because she lived only a couple of doors from the school, we could hear the volleys as her mother shoved her out the door.

Sleepy was Peanut's brother. Almost ambitious, and possessing a snide sense of humor, he asked on the first day of class, "At our prom, do we all dance with Sad Eyes and Lala?" He dressed well, worked when pressed, but could be a real jerk at times.

Wino, a Puerto Rican transplant from New York, told me as soon as he showed up, "I'm dumb. I didn't even finish first grade. I don't know nothin' about school. The police didn't even try to find me when I went AWOL at youth authority. They knew I would do something stupid, and they would just catch me."

What bound these teens as a group was that, for reasons from boredom to poverty to anxiety and mild retardation, they had all slipped out of the net and were now floundering. For many reasons, all had let go of the community's towline to adulthood. And, being children, they simply stayed stranded, got into trouble, developed addictions and made things much worse for themselves.

8

I wrote letters to professors and nonprofits asking for help, and therapist interns from Cal State L.A. appeared one morning asking if they could volunteer. I had never met anyone who had attended therapy. I wasn't sure what occurred, but I assumed it was salubrious. They set up in my office for a few hours twice a week, and the kids could choose to go in and talk to them.

Happy came out of the room on one occasion, pulled me aside, and told me in a low tone: "The lady says I can talk about anything. 'I asked her, even about you and me making ... making sex?' And she didn't get mad. She said we could even talk about that! Homeboy, I never talked to no lady like this."

The experience allowed kids to know that seeing a therapist was pleasant and didn't mean you were crazy. It was one more place to get help.

I called the education department at USC, and the director of student teaching sent me top-of-the-line trainees. The kids loved them. One student teacher was very interested in the kids, so she gave them a lot of extra time. Several had crushes on her. They couldn't understand why I wasn't making a move. "Art's afraid of that stuff," they would chorus once she was out the door.

The bakery let us have a weeks' worth of bread on Monday mornings. Coaches volunteered from a local basketball league, and the students said that if they saw gang members from other neighborhoods, it would be war. But that was followed by "Will we get uniforms?"

Even the mayor offered help. His "Task Force on Youth" consisted of young people who met on the top floor of city hall and advised one of his deputies. We rode the elevator with the mayor on a few occasions, and for meetings we got to sit in big chairs around a long, polished table. It gave my students a different peer group and another identity to feel part of.

One of the most powerful interventions resulted from a small gesture. The police officers of the Newton Division patrolled the local area. Over several years, they had arrested every student in the auditorium. These aversive interactions were frequent: the police pulled the kids over if they were several in a car. The police chased them out of the local park, picked them up for not being in school, stopped them if they appeared high or if it was after curfew.

I drove to the station before the first day of school and met with the local police sergeant. I let him know there would be this gathering of delinquents at the community center and why. We talked for a while, and he said that in juvenile hall, most of the kids couldn't read the letters their girlfriends sent them. He hoped we would focus on basics.

One morning, early in the semester, the sergeant and one of his officers stopped their car in front of the school. They walked into the auditorium, creating a tense chill as they stood in the back for a few minutes. I am sure the students assumed one of them was about to be detained.

After looking over the crowd, the two officers began approaching students. They asked what they were working on, offered small positive comments. The two officers made it to a table where Sharkey and Lil'

Man were learning to read. They sat down, one on each end, and asked each to read for them. The cops helped them sound out some of their words, and I could see that Lil' Man and Sharkey were trying hard to impress.

For the rest of the school year, the police checked in several days a week. They looked over student work, asked them to explain what they were learning, complimented them. The police sergeant most enjoyed reading with Sharkey and Lil' Man. He would listen, pointing out how much they were improving, and now and then dropping his arm around a shoulder.

9

I received a call from the owner of a Kentucky Fried Chicken in Beverly Hills. Playboy's older brother had worked for him, and now Playboy himself had applied. The owner wanted a reference and asked about the school. He was a Lebanese gentleman with a thick accent who asked very good questions. He said he would like to hire my students to give them experience, but under one condition. He would hire Playboy first, as he seemed a natural leader, and Playboy would be responsible for his friends. If money disappeared, or a worker didn't show, it was going to come out of Playboy's pocket.

The owner, whom I never met in person, told me, "I'm a businessman, a realist. A boy who is used to trouble doesn't become an angel overnight. I'll work with them, and they'll get second chances, but it will cost their friend."

Playboy agreed and brought Casper in for an interview. The owner hired him. By end of the month, several gang members were frying chicken, working the register, cleaning the bathrooms and politely asking people in Beverly Hills if they wanted biscuits or coleslaw.

The last one hired was Happy. It was his first job, and the day of the interview he sat in class petrified all morning. He was even worse the first day of work. But he caught on.

The boys watched each other and made sure no one stole anything. Since

Playboy was an assistant manager, he kept the others in line.

In February, Happy quit. He came to class one day and said that it was too many hours and he bad to concentrate on his education. He was a hefty boy, with a thin mustache that made him look like a Greek fisherman. He told me once that when he got high, he just started running, sometimes went for a mile or two, and that it felt freeing. He had an innocence that didn't match his size. My heart warmed to hear him walk in with a pressed t-shirt and talk about the importance of an education over a part-time job.

Casper was also working long hours, sometimes closing during the week and getting home at one or two in the morning. He started missing school, but it was obvious the money was helping him and his family. I had been so happy with his previous work that I leaned on him about missing school, told him he had to be on time, or he couldn't come at all. It was stupid of me. We had developed a mutual admiration, and now there was this adversarial quality to our relationship. He got an attitude because I got an attitude.

He opted for the job and decided to quit school, but he kept coming around, trying to sit in, saying he could pass our tests, wanting his grades. What I should have done was work around the fact that he was coming home late and therefore getting up late. I could have assigned him extra take-home work or given him partial but important credit for a partial day. It could have been a lesson in managing competing concerns.

Instead, I took it personally and boxed him in. Fortunately, he gave *me* a second chance.

10

Casper started school like most of his peers—illiterate and full of attitude. To teach, I had to lob him nice, fat slow balls, and enjoy watching him get some wood on them. Breaking the world into big, recognizable pieces, with patience and repetition, allowed Casper to get a handle on this world. It showed in his attendance, in his growing engagement and his eagerness to take tests.

There was no curve and there were no "good kids" to compete with at El Santo

Niño. It didn't matter that what we studied should have been learned in primary school. We made it simple and fun, and if you put in the effort, you were rewarded for it.

Sharky struggled with the alphabet, and reading went something like, "The . . . ho . . . horse . . . house . . . for . . . what's this word?"

"Sharon. It's a name."

"I don't understand this story. It don't make sense."

Lil Man was worse than Sharky. He knew the first half of the alphabet, but after that it got dicey. He had no idea how to put a vowel and consonant together to make a syllable. Lil'Man spoke little, and never looked anyone in the eye. He kept a blue cap tight over his Jheri curls and dropped over his eyes. He'd only been in our neighborhood for a couple months. The local principal had already expelled him, and he was supposed to take a bus to the Metro Continuation School downtown.

His grandfather didn't think he would go, so he signed him up, "Where the Mexican boys who cause trouble go."

He never said anything about a previous gang affiliation, but the blue cap told everyone he'd been allied with an African American gang. Where we lived, Eighteenth Street was the monster entity to fear and avoid. We never thought about Bloods and Crips.

Nietzsche said, "Nothing is as expensive as a start." Starting is slow, and foundations take time. I sat with Lil Man and Sharky after school and said, "You guys can't read, and that's not your fault. Nobody's taken the time to teach you. I'm going to teach you. It might take the year, doesn't matter. To get an 'A,' your job is to learn to read. Everyone has a goal in this room, and this is your goal. If you don't learn, then I guess I don't know what I'm doing."

I typed out three sheets with simple phonetic combinations of vowels and consonants, hundreds of them. The first sheet began with the syllables, "co, co, la, la, da, da, ba, ba, be, be "

I put the first sheet in front of them and said, "Follow me." After a few minutes, I placed a simple book in front of them, and we read together. I took the lead on these exercises with enthusiasm to make sure there was little opportunity for embarrassment. They read out loud throughout the day and always with someone listening.

Yogi was good for that. He lived behind the school and came over to brush up on the basics, maybe get a diploma, explore what else might be out there for him. He was a kind, big bear of a boy, and all the kids liked him. He would sit and listen to Sharky and Lil' Man read. So did Sad Eyes and Lala, and sometimes Droopy or Smiley as it became normal to hear their staccato, struggling voices in the background. Tired or bored students would often ask if they could listen to Sharky or Lil' Man for a while.

It was in January, five months after our first day of school. The class was drawing the organs of the body. Spanky and Casper were with my co-teacher Juan Esqueda matching countries to pictures from *National Geographic*. Sharky was reading how the slaves were transported across the Atlantic.

He was sitting next to me, his focus on a picture book, and I heard him blow out a perfect set of notes. With absolute ease, I heard him say out loud, "They were sick and crowded. Many people died on the ships."

He stopped and glanced up at me. "I don't read all slow and stopping anymore, eh Homes?" He looked a little startled with himself.

"No, you don't. You got it down, Sharky."

Lil Man never gave that kind of proclamation. As he gained competence, he began to lift his cap back so he could look you in the eye, and in the mornings, he would claim a seat nearer the front of class.

There were kids in gangs who did violence to others and to themselves, and there were those who feared it. They were shadows in the gang, neither stopping nor participating in the violence.

Smiley had dreams. He was curious and kind. It unsettled him that other gang members were "destructive." I remember fondly that he made a bench of wood crates for us to sit on while I waited for the bus after school. He hid it behind a tree and would pull it out when he walked me to the bus stop at the end of the day.

One afternoon, I had to close the Catholic community center, where I worked in the evenings, to rush his dog to the vet. He bad asked a neighbor to clip the little mutt's ears so it would look like a Doberman. But by the time I got there, the dog was butchered and bleeding to death.

"I want to save its life," he told me. We drove to the vet, who put the dog to sleep. The vet told me, "I see many of these things, and they're awful. But if I went to court or got into each case, I'd have no time to keep my business. You know what I mean?" I was angry about the dog, and he was letting me know that he wasn't into pursuing the butcher.

Smiley was full of regrets. "I didn't know, Homie. You know, I just wanted it to look tough. I didn't know. The man told me he knew how to cut ears. He jacked up my dog."

Smiley had two siblings in college, a third who played in a band, and two hardworking, decent parents. They owned a home that had been carefully maintained.

Yet no one, not in school or at home, had noticed that Smiley was completely uneducated, that schooling had left no trace on him. He was unable to do any mathematics at all, not a stitch of any calculation.

He could not provide you any historical facts or the name of the planet he inhabited. Yet he was in the ninth grade and had attended the local elementary and junior high school. He had learned to hide and manage impressions with kindness and cleverness.

When Smiley began the year at El Santo Niño, he could read at a fifth-grade level, which, except for Playboy and Pirate, was exceptional for our group. In Smiley's case, literacy wasn't problematic. Reading came easy to him. His biggest and fundamental deficit was the kind of thinking a person needs in order to do math. In the same way that Lil Man and Sharky hardly knew their alphabet, Smiley could do no arithmetic except to count on his fingers.

Watching Smiley struggle with arithmetic, I learned much about the relation of one mental process with the others. Smiley obviously had intelligence, and he was observant. When I had to go to court over a problem with a landlord, he advised me to take a lawyer with me.

"I can't afford one."

"Anybody with a suit and a briefcase, Homeboy. He just has to look like one. That'll make 'em settle with you."

Then, why the lack of knowledge? Apparently, his inability to hold numbers in head and to understand a concept like multiplication also hampered his efforts to put together other kinds of information. He knew about the world in bits, but they did not come together into wholes that made sense. He knew about the Earth, and he knew he lived on a planet. He just didn't know that Earth was the planet he lived on.

Smiley had difficulty putting two and two together whether it involved numbers or other strings of information.

The only solution to his difficulty with numbers was to imagine what it would be like to think like him. We worked on addition and subtraction for months. The daily routine began with picturing birds: "Smiley, close your eyes and imagine five pigeons."

"Where are they?"

"On a telephone wire. Have one fly away. Can you picture the ones that are still on the wire?"

Guiding his thought processes in this direct manner changed something. Holding images or ideas constant while manipulating them became easier. By year's end, he was picking up fractions with ease—he could now put together disparate pieces of information and see their relatedness

Interestingly, this facility led to an interest in politics. He became the most vocal member of the group we took to the Mayor's Task Force on Youth. Smiley increasingly became bothered by the inconsistencies and contradictions in the world around him.

11

Even with the twenty dollar per month student tuition, our small budget left only a few hundred dollars for supplies, so I went on a hunt for free books. They had to be at various reading levels, with lots of pictures, and touching on as many subjects as possible. We received what we needed from L.A.'s Central Public Library and a well-known private school.

Sharky and I made a trip to the La Cañada-Flintridge Sacred Heart Academy for Girls, an elite boarding school where my brother helped with elaborate theatrical productions. The head of the drama department arranged with the school librarian for me to inherit not only their used books, but she arranged for several elementary schools to do the same. We picked up the elementary school donations, and afterward made our way to the boarding school. The last collection waited for us at the top of a La Cañada mountain.

When we arrived, a tall, exceptionally beautiful and gracious Asian student helped us with our task. She was affluent, well-spoken and all confidence. She made quite an impression. Sharky was wearing his oversized white t-shirt and starched gray khakis. He carried boxes behind her, bobbing up and down with that funny walk he perfected and now did without thinking. It all took about an hour.

We were both tired and quiet on the way down the hill. Sharky seemed pensive, and I asked what he was thinking.

"I'd like to have a girlfriend like that Chinita. Clean and, you know, nice."

We had both been nursing similar thoughts.

"I don't know, Sharky. You might have to change a few things for a girl like that."

"I know, Homes. It's like my friend, Tomas. In his house, he got all kinds of trophies for him and his dad. Baseball and football."

He was looking straight forward as he talked, watching the beautiful houses, one after the other as we descended the curved, single lane road.

"Girls like that Chinita, Homes, they want a guy who has trophies."

I didn't argue.

The Optimist Oratorical Society sponsored a speech contest every year. It went all the way to nationals, and I had participated in night grade. I called the owner of the donut shop who had been my sponsor and asked if I could enter a couple of my kids.

Once I explained the nature of our school, he was excited to sponsor us. I asked Playboy and Lala to compete in the men's and women's divisions. They were both cocky and verbal.

We worked and reworked their speeches, timed them, and rehearsed them for weeks. The day of the contest, I put on my suit and drove to the school. Lala wore an elegant, dark dress and was ready to go. It was time to leave, and Playboy came huffing in at the last minute, wearing his suit but saying that he couldn't go, that there was going to be fight and he had to be there, that the fight was important and he couldn't let the gang down.

Of course, there was no big fight. He was just scared, as I remembered being. I told him to please cut out the bullshit and take care of business. He noticed Lala already in the car and perfectly composed. That was all it took. We were on the way.

We arrived to an auditorium in a prestigious hotel. The competition was the best of public and private schools: student body presidents and high GPA types. The judges knew this, and when they introduced Lala and Playboy, I appreciated the tone of support in their voices.

The other orators were excellent, as they had to be. Playboy's turn came first. I pressed his shoulder, and Sad Eyes, who had come along to be supportive, whispered, "You'll be all right."

He was amazing. He started stiff-shouldered and speaking too fast, but he caught himself, and from midpoint on, he was animated and only looked at his notes to guide himself—not getting stuck on them as I feared. The audience was rapt as he delivered his speech, "I Am a Gang Member." He walked back looking like he'd made it through a minefield. I was glad I had forced him to do this.

"How was I, Homeboy?"

"Everybody loved it. You've got a good chance."

Lala was last of the women's division, and the last of the evening. She had been given time to get plenty nervous. She followed a demure girl from Bethune Junior High who gave a polished, well-choreographed speech, an orator obviously comfortable in these settings.

Lala, who wasn't a small girl, and even in a dress looked tough, squeezed my hand as she got up. "Wish me luck, Arturo." Her speech was just as good as the girl before her, and she knew it. She walked back with chin up and a confident stride.

The limit for speeches was three minutes. Both Lala and Playboy went over by ten to fifteen seconds, and that cost them points. Against opponents this well prepared, such a lapse eliminated a chance at first place.

However, the emcee announced with enthusiasm that Playboy and Lala had taken second in their respective divisions. They received extended applause as they collected their trophies.

After the event, one of the judges walked over to us and confirmed that both had been within range of first place. I told the judge this was my fault, which was true, for timing their speeches to close to the limit. The judge responded that they had given speeches on par with the top students in the city and should keep competing.

At that moment, I regretted not making a stronger effort to invite parents. I had been afraid with family in the audience their nerves would get the better of them.

Lala and Playboy collected their trophies and certificates. They exchanged a round of handshakes before we stepped out into a lovely March evening.

"Let's go somewhere good for dinner, a nice place. What about it, Art?" asked Playboy.

"If everyone wants to."

"I'll treat everyone," he offered.

"How about me and you treat? We'll split it.

"That's cool, Homeboy."

The four of us went to a restaurant in Pasadena and enjoyed a late dinner and good conversation. We drove home feeling accomplished and strong.

12

I had recovered my van, stripped of everything but frame and engine. The boys helped me put some carpet in it. After a little rewiring and tinkering, it was hardy enough to serve on days when we needed a break. We'd make sandwiches from stuff we had in the kitchen, crowd into three vans and take trips to museums, a movie or a part of town to explore.

Some trips were better planned. We visited places that made ideas palpable. Since we had been covering history and world religions, I contacted Buddhist monasteries, Jewish synagogues, and Greek Orthodox churches to make an itinerary.

Pirate decided to skip the world religion trip and go home. He was in a horrid mood. He could be a pain, so I wasn't going to push it. He was verbal and bright and could have performed decently in a public school, except he was always angry, wouldn't work, and was stoned most the time. His parents were involved in the community, and when the police told them about the school, they brought him over.

They warned me he would be stubborn. The first few weeks, he mostly came to class and fell asleep on the benches along the auditorium walls. He took part in a discussion now and then by raising his head and arguing a point. We allowed it, as pushing him had only frustrated everyone else.

You would think that allowing Pirate to get away with this would have set off a rebellion of copycat behaviors. And yes, one student tried to mimic him and sleep against the wall, but he backed off at the quick "don't even try it" look from my co-teacher. Kids are intuitive: they assumed that Pirate had a problem. He was their friend, and they wanted to believe he would eventually come around.

Pirate continued his routine for several weeks. When we didn't fight him or put him down, he became bored and gradually participated in more of the school day. By the end of the year, we had almost forgotten about sleep-against-wall Pirate.

But today, he was in one of those moods, and I wasn't going to beg him.

Sharky compulsively drew on things, including my van if I didn't watch him. He was always apologetic and willing to scrub it off, but prevention was better. I made him empty his pockets before getting in. At UCLA, the graffiti he drew in the parking lot cost us fifty dollars.

"Sorry, Homes," he said, "My hand just starts making the neighborhood."·

Our first stop was the Cathedral of Saint Sophia, a beautiful Greek Orthodox church, with its huge dome from which Mary looked down from a Byzantine sky. It impressed them as the largest mural they had ever contemplated. The kids were reverent enough and when the long-bearded priest said "hello," it left an image to which they could attach the word Greek Orthodox.

At a small synagogue in the Fairfax district, a rabbi discussed the Holocaust with them. A group of Orthodox men came in with their long coats, hats and beards to help with the presentation.

Afterward, we ate lunch at Canter's deli. I ordered the least expensive thing on the menu, a round of matzo ball soup for the group. They all had the same question, "Why did those guys all dress like Abraham Lincoln?" I really had no idea, but it was fun to see. The soup filled us up, even though each bowl had just one big meatball in it.

For the Buddhist experience, we stopped at an old, two-story house in East Hollywood that served as a monastery. Ben, an American convert, met us in the parking lot and told us that the priest would meet us in the meditation room upstairs. In the large atrium, we sat on mats in a circle, our backs against the wall.

"You think Homeboy's going to do kung fu?" Casper wondered out loud.

Trying to get comfortable, Ben asked, "You all come from the same school?"

"Yeah," Joker said. "From Gangster High."

"Have some *respeto,* fool," Casper shot back, before turning to Ben and saying, "*Dispense*, he don't know how to act."

They were used to talking to each other that way, and it didn't escalate.

Ben continued, ignoring them, "Master Che is a Buddhist monk. Do you have ideas about what that might be?"

"It's like from China," Sad Eyes said.

"They believe in reincarnation, or something like that, Homey," Sparky added.

"Like when you come back as animals cause you're bad," Goofy said, "and you pray to the Buddha man."

Ben smiled, satisfied with their answers. "That's all correct. It looks like you've been studying."

I felt pretty good. They were giving a decent account of themselves.

The Monk appeared in a black robe with something like meditation or rosary beads around his neck. He was Korean, short, probably in his fifties, with a shaved head, and he walked with a cane. He bowed to the kids, some of whom sort of bowed backed from their seats. Ben introduced him, "This is Master Che. He is the monk who leads this monastery."

Playboy made a crack, and the monk immediately said, "You speak again, no permission, and I break your back forty times." He was obviously aware of the popularity of the show Kung Fu, and he was willing to play with the stereotype. The threat was enough to calm them down. I like that he had an edgy sense of humor.

"Master Che can see an object coming from behind," Ben explained. "He reacts in a moment because he is always in the present."

The monk cut him off. "I teach you Buddhism. What is this?" He rapped twice on the floor with his cane.

"It's the floor," the group mumbled, knowing something was up.

"No, that is its *name*. What is *this!*" and two sharp taps followed.

Playboy engaged him. "It's wood."

"No! That is the *material* it is made from. What is *THIS!"*

"You walk on it," Playboy answered with more energy.

"That is its *function*. What is *THIS!"* He tapped his cane several times in a precise rhythm as he stared at the group.

"It's whatever you think it is," Lala shot back.

"So, what is it?" Psycho said, losing his patience.

"It *IS!*," responded the monk.

"The sound?" several students said at once.

"No!" Master Che shook his head.

"I get it," Playboy said over the group. "It just is."

The monk regarded him with cheerful eyes. "Yes! Now, you are Buddhist! You will be happy!"

With that, the monk bowed and excused himself.

13

Woody was stout and muscular, a bit of a bad ass in the gang. He didn't attend for the first few weeks because a rival gang had jumped him and left him for dead. When he finally showed up to class, his arm was still in a cast and his jaws were wired shut. He had to talk through his teeth.

This event triggered a transformation. Being near death, turning sixteen and going through all that pain made him aware of his vulnerability. He began to reflect on the life he wanted. This might have gone nowhere, but in a small and safe atmosphere, and with sealed jaws, he listened and worked.

As with most of our students, Woody arrived barely literate, unable to write except in an unpunctuated ramble, and he had little knowledge of the outside world. But he learned quickly, and in weeks gained an ease with structuring ideas and words into sentences and paragraphs, something that was taking other students' months.

"It makes sense, when you do it this way," and he showed me an essay with three paragraphs and periods at the end of sentences.

"It's not easy, Woody. You've got talent for writing."

He grew curious about the world, eating up stories about other countries and cultures. At midyear, he had a beautiful, hardworking girlfriend who wasn't in the gang. His jaw braces came off, and he decided he wanted to go back to Jefferson

High School. Two weeks later, he returned and asked to rejoin our class. He said there were too many gang members at the high school and that trouble would be easy to fall into.

I had missed him. Later that year, my brother and several friends organized a mountain religious retreat that most of the gang attended, along with the kids from St. Vincent's youth group. It was strange retreat, a lot of highs and lows, and on Saturday night two of the Clanton boys went off and broke windows, turned over beds and went a bit haywire.

Early the next morning, I found Woody sweeping the glass. He had put things back together. He told me his father had a janitorial service that he helped with, and he knew how to clean up quickly. He and several members of the team sat around and talked while the rest of the campers still slept. He was embarrassed for the gang, and it was obvious that he did not consider himself part of their activity. It was also obvious, as we all stood there, that he was making a transition.

By June, his clothing had changed to a pressed shirt and khaki pants that did not look entirely cholo. He hung out with his girlfriend, was helping his father more, had bought a car, and was studying for his driver's license.

At the end of the school year, and the last time I saw him, he said, "I know what you're trying to do with us. Mainly one thing I can thank you for, and that was the retreat." He didn't say anything more about it, but he wanted me to know that "I know only one thing, and that's to work. That's all my father taught me, and that's what I know."

He was now back on to a different life. A couple of years later, I had lunch with Sharkey to talk about his bookkeeping course at the Job Corp. Sharkey told me that Woody had made a business with his dad and was being a good father to his newborn.

14

The years gradually transformed Happy into a man with high-achieving children, a fine marriage, and steady employment running a warehouse. I had not seen him for ten years when a reporter for the LA. Reader asked if I could find any of the students for her to interview.

We went through old address books and located parents who had stayed in the neighborhood. This led to a conversation with Happy's mother, who informed me that they had tried to find me for his wedding and that I would be proud of who he had become.

I was proud. Happy offered to host a small reunion for the reporter at his home. I understood that part of his joy would be showing off his new house, purchased in the old neighborhood and a great source of satisfaction.

"This is my house!" he told me as he patted his heart with his hand. In the bedroom was a computer for his two children, and the little girl was wearing a patch to correct a lazy eye that impeded her reading ability. Both children were in a private school. "They were having problems, getting behind, and I heard that a Catholic school would be better. What do you think?"

I thought I might as well be talking to any middle-class parent out on the West Side, except I was in South Central Los Angeles.

How Happy got there involved hitting the mat a few times but getting back up for another round. He went through AA and guarded his sobriety with all the care of a good AA participant. His wife stayed with him through the tumbles.

He brought out the homework I used to give him, and he reminded me that I forced him to read the newspaper.

"Now I read the newspaper every day. I can tell you about Iraq, NAFTA, the elections."

As a boy, you would have thought him distracted and learning disabled. As an adult, Happy displayed cleverness, wisdom, humor, and a fast wit that kept me at attention.

Happy still claimed the gang. To him, they and the affiliation they shared were the friends of his youth, they were his memories. Most of them still lived in the neighborhood. They had baptized each other's children, gone camping together, grieved for those fallen into homelessness or long-term incarceration, and sometimes buried each other.

Happy would have thought me crazy for assuming he would participate in a drive-by, commit a criminal act, or be an irresponsible parent. He thought the current generation was worse, and he lectured the local gang members, forgetting the severity of his own misadventures. Happy understood that the problem was never the gang itself, but the specific behaviors in which they engaged, and which destroyed many of their lives. It is these behaviors he had risen above.

Other gang members also managed to find proper lives. Playboy became a career officer in the military. Smiley raised British Tumblers, a fine breed of bird, which he sold and placed into competitions. Sad Girl, Lala and Heidi all finished school and attained varying amounts of higher education. Joker married, had good children and a job he enjoyed. He and Happy took their kids camping together. Yogi still worked on cars and had a family. Sleepy and Psycho moved out of the neighborhood and gave good accounts of themselves.

Others struggled.

Sharky, after completing a bookkeeping course, did not find work. The deaths of his older brothers proved difficult. He found little jobs, attempted to be a good parent to his and Juanita's children, and often had to beg, borrow and sell drugs to get by.

Casper died. He had recently exited prison, and while walking to Happy's house to watch a pay-per-view fight, he fell upon some young gang members from another neighborhood. They gunned him down. Happy's mother shared with me how, earlier that day, he had been at her house saying, "I'm glad for Happy. I want to try to put my life together like he did."

Popeye and Pirate struggled with addictions. They still lived at home, always teetering between making it and bottoming out.

Goofy was also dead.

Droopy eventually killed someone and will never leave prison.

Droopy made me particularly sad. I still pictured him learning to waltz for a quinceañera. I can hear the lecture I gave him for taking my car one day without permission. I can remember his voice saying, "I'm a bad boy," in a slow stupor as Sister Natalia hovered over his silver-coated face. I remember being surprised that he could open a remote control, take out the transistors, solder in new ones, and make it work. I know now that a little Ritalin, a special school, some anger management and decent therapy, and he would be out today, and someone else would be alive.

Crime is down across the nation—gangs are no longer a major issue—but alienated or marginalized kids still act out and self-harm in other ways. For the troubled kids at El Santo Niño, I know what decided their fates: the patient resourcefulness of their parents, schools that either supported or rejected them, and the availability of people who understood how to treat their particular problems and addictions. Simple, elusive stuff.

If they had the fortune to find this combination of adults, then a coherent, sustained guidance into adulthood developed. For a minute, El Santo Nino provided that supportive track to growing up. Those students who managed to find it after El Santo Nino are alive, sober, and enjoying this day. For those who did not, growing up was stunted and they went back to wandering the periphery of their village, struggling for a way back in. As Happy told me years ago, "I should be dead. I kept messing up. But my parents, my wife, everybody. They kept trying. They just didn't give up on me. No one gave up on me."

INDIAN COUNTRY

Part 3

15

Through word of mouth and some writing, the story of El Santo Niño found resonance in both inner-city and rural schools, and I was invited to share across the country. But it was in Indian Country that I saw what is possible when a community decides to support its most difficult children.

After a magazine interview, I received a call from a Steve Saffron, the grandfather of the humor-for-healing movement, and he told me that his therapist in California had read about the school. She felt that

Steve and I should meet. We talked on the phone a bit, and he said, "Come stay with me a few days. I have a feeling about this."

My aging Australian Shepard rode with me from L.A. to Phoenix, and we stayed for several days in Steve's home. He was a wise, funny and exceptionally energetic man. On the first day, he said, "I want you to go with me to the Pima-Maricopa reservation. I do a lot of humor workshops with their people. They've been family to me since I left Ohio after the war. You need to meet them."

We spent the rest of the week making friends on the reservation, talking to people in their homes, meeting the elders and leaders. I left with an invitation to give some workshops. Eventually, I received an offer to help build their first secondary school. They had moved a set of bungalows from other parts of the reservation, and I would inherit this setting to seed an eventual junior and senior high school.

It was a critical time on the reservation. The gang issue had taken many Pima-Maricopa children. Without a school on the reservation, the students were bused to Mesa, and few of them attended or graduated. I have a clear memory of Ivan Malik, the president of the community, asking me, "Build an Indian High School, not a white high school on a reservation. Help us create Indian teachers and our own curriculum, and then leave."

It was a beautiful invitation and the privilege of a lifetime.

But first, we needed the community to accept President Malik's vision. They were tired of promises, tired of people from the outside coming in with their non-solutions. And they hungered to do things in a manner that made sense for a tribal people. I needed to listen to what they yearned for, help them create it—and then leave. These were their children, and this was their history, their fight.

Over the next few months, as I began to learn the obstacles they were up against—and there were many—I began to appreciate an advantage of tribal life which the off-reservation could only envy.

What they were up against was history. Their river and its ancient canals had supported Indian agriculture for centuries. When it was diverted to create the Salt River Canal, a wide-spread famine took place, and they lost their livelihood. In time, only non-Indian farmers had the means to tap the canal and Pima cotton was grown on land leased from the Pima, but not by them.

I asked why they lived in trailers, and they explained the obvious: you can't take out a mortgage on federal land. Banks cannot repossess it. As one elder explained, "It's called a reservation because it is reserved for us, but when we are no more, it will go to the government. That's been the plan all along."

Tribal members lived in mobile homes and trailers that could be financed. Building a house with cash from ground up was as prohibitive for them as it would be for any of us.

There were few phones at the time. Cell towers had not come to the reservation, and to obtain a land line required paying for telephones poles from Scottsdale to the home. The cost would have been forty thousand dollars. Cash. And with few phones, communication with Mesa school teachers and administrators was non-existent. Their kids knew this, and the consequences were predictable.

But still, in terms of their children, they had a key advantage for the future.

As one Pima probation officer explained, "We can't escape our kids. When a kid in Phoenix gets picked up, he disappears to who knows where. And the family has probably moved to another neighborhood by the time he gets out. He doesn't really belong to anyone but his mom. But jailed Indian kids live in that little building where we all see them. There is no forgetting. And when they get out, they come right back to all of us."

A small tribe couldn't have a child become a fifty-year burden to their family and community. They needed to believe that every kid could be turned around, and to that end, few ideas we're off the table.

After many meetings, some of them contentious, a plan developed, and the tribe voted to give me a chance. We found a Navajo vice-principal who was an award-winning artist and former professional fighter. He had many strengths I lacked. People with experience in traditional crafts showed up to teach, and being a charter school, we were able to hire them. Pima college students filled our aide ranks, and in short time they would become Pima teachers. We replaced social studies with Native Studies, found a fluent Pima speaker on the Tohono'Odham reservation to teach language and bought enough musical instruments for a full band program. Just as important, we had connected our school with every agency on the reservation, and with the elders, the police and the business community. We let it be known that our purpose was to educate every tribal student, including the gang-involved and the most problematic.

A final meeting was held to explain the vision to the community. Tribal leaders and our staff took questions, and it went well until the last few minutes. As we were about to start the potluck, a tall, older teen with a menacing scowl raised his hand. He was with a group of gang members who had stood against the back wall for the two hours, saying nothing.

He was well known to the community and considered a leader of his group. When he was called upon to speak, the gang leader said, "This was a good meeting for you.

Everybody is excited now. But you all know this isn't going to happen. This only works if we want it to work. And you all know that WE don't want it to work. It's just another waste of time."

What he said mattered. He was the problem we were trying to solve. The room froze, with the boys in the back staring down the speakers around the podium. What saved us was a tribal elder who was serving as a councilman. Mr. Largo stood up from a seat at the front of the room and turned around to face the young man.

"Mario," he said. "You're a teenager, and your job is to make life difficult for us. You've done a good job at that. But we are adults, and *our* job is to raise you. And son, believe me, we don't need your permission to do that. I'm not asking you to like what you're going to do. But you are going to do it."

Those were the last official words of the meeting. A blessing was offered, and everyone went for a plate of food.

Mr. Largo walked over and spoke to Mario, introduced me, and asked if I would give the young man and his brother a ride home. In the car, the gang leader said something so honest it stayed with me till this day. As I dropped him off in front of his trailer, he told me "Everyone in my life has always been afraid of me. Even when I was little. I like that Mr. Largo isn't afraid of me. Maybe this time the grown-ups won't quit and run."

16

I was invited to a winter Pow-wow for community youth. It had been in progress all day, and it was getting time for the last dances.

Steve Saffron was with me, and he pointed to something important.

"Arturo, see that man. He's the chief of police."

The chief of police was dancing in a procession with several kids who by now I recognized as the most challenging young men on the reservation, obvious gang members. The chief had linked arms with two of them, and they were circulating to the music of drum and song as we all watched. One of the tribal elders, and a good friend of Steve's, turned to me and repeated what I'd heard from the probation officer.

"We can't send our youth away or blame someone else like you can. These kids are a part of us."

At the end of the Pow-Wow, the police chief stood with the chairman of the celebration and gave the following blessing:

"We pray for our children, including those who sleep tonight behind bars. We love them also."

I could not imagine the police in Los Angeles sharing publicly in a sentiment like this, but it reflected a reality of Indian life. Troubled, difficult and criminal youth on the reservation were not the enemies, but the sons and daughters of the community. The task force meetings that followed that

Pow-wow were not cold conversations about suppression and longer sentences, but a communal sharing about how to best discipline, nurture, protect and involve the most lost and prodigal of their children. As cliché as it sounds, this was going to take a village.

17

The temporary junior and senior high school consisted of old buildings that were moved to a corner of the desert reservation. Plumbing had been connected, no small or inexpensive task when cutting through underground caliche. Telephones and electrical utilities were likewise installed. For what remained, the tribe allowed students to build their own school.

With supervision from the guys at Public Works, students painted, dug out forms, buried water lines for sprinklers, seeded winter grasses and carved out the holes for two dozen trees.

If you don't know the desert, for several months a year, children can't use parks because they'll fry on the slides. Dogs get shoes if they're walking on sidewalks. We needed shade for outdoor lunch tables, meetings and gatherings, and the best, long-term shade came from trees. We purchased twenty Mesquites. I was new to the desert, but the staff told me it was the fastest growing of the desert trees, and the nursery showed me pictures with branches that stretched wide against the sun.

One of the clans on the reservation, the Manuel's, were involved in the effort to hold onto the Pima language and pass on their traditions. Alice Manuel said we should invite a medicine woman to bless the school and students. At that time, there was no longer a medicine woman on this reservation, but Alice had a good relationship with the medicine woman from

Gila River. She arranged to bring her on the first day of school. She would bless every student with a sacred brushing.

When the day arrived, students were gathered inside our largest building. Teachers waited outside and supervised the groups waiting still to enter. I busied myself with the landscaping, untying trees that had just arrived and tying the new bougainvillea against our fence.

The brushing ceremony took hours. All our teacher aides were Pima and two of the teachers were Pueblo and Navajo, and being Native, they also partook in the ceremony. As the aides and teachers came out, they said it was the first time they had seen such discipline from these kids. The young men and women stood for several hours without talking or complaining in a warm auditorium lit by window light.

The medicine woman attended to one student after next. She asked each to say his or her name and what was in their heart. A young aide said she could hear kids confessing fears for family or that they wouldn't be able to stay out of jail or pass classes. They expressed regrets, hopes that a diabetic parent not die or that they could overcome an addiction. Each child whispered their confession, and afterward the medicine woman brushed them with desert sage and blessed them.

The children in jail waited for their brushing as well, and she walked over to the detention facilities and offered the same blessings before being done for the day.

When it was over and the children had gone home, I was still gardening. It was the most relaxing aspect of being a principal. The campus was quiet, with a few teachers working in their classrooms. I saw the medicine woman walking toward me with her son. He was a professional landscaper by trade, but he accompanied his aging mother for these ceremonies.

I had just finished digging and was preparing to lay in the first of the mesquites. I stood up with dirty hands and she shook mine as did her son. She asked me what I was planning.

"Shade. I'm from California, so I asked, and everyone said to plant mesquites. I want the kids to eat outside like a normal school."

She looked at the metal rods I had purchased to support each tree.

"Have you heard of monsoons, Mr. Arturo."

"I was caught in one last year. It almost lifted me off my bicycle."

"You're planting in the monsoon season."

"I know, but we need shade trees."

"The monsoons will take out your trees. And a mesquite is more a bush than a tree—do you know that Mr. Arturo?"

I told her that I'd seen mesquites that were tall and had wide branches. And she answered that I hadn't see this in the desert, where they grow naturally, and are bent from years withstanding the winds without breaking.

"If you want the mesquite to be a straight tree," she said, "and you're going to plant in a monsoon, what you're doing now will not work."

Her son then helped me hammer stakes in a circle around the first tree and tie them tight to the trunk. I asked her how many stakes we needed.

"The desert storms can come from any direction. Anywhere the tree is without a stake, that's where it will fall. The desert doesn't care."

Once we had made a tight perfect circle, we talked more about the mesquite as a bush. I told her I absolutely needed it to be a tree.

"It can be, you've seen them. But in nature it survives by bending to the ground. Its trunk stays bent to survive. If you want it to grow straight, it needs something stronger that itself to hold onto."

The medicine woman told me to go back to the nursery and bring back hardwood poles while the ground was still soft. She would wait.

An hour later, her son and I returned. The nursery owner said he had wondered how I was going to plant mesquites in this season, and he sold us some expensive, treated timber.

The medicine woman directed me to bury a hardwood pole next to the tree we had staked from the roots to its present height. We tied the pole and mesquite to each other with a strong, natural twine, and made sure the pole was also tied to the stakes.

"Now, the poles strength, because it is mature, will be the mesquites strength. Don't ever remove it. The mesquite is young and will grow quickly. Its trunk will wrap itself around the old wood, and someday you won't see it, but it will always be there."

We did that, and when completed, I had a tree that was straight, steady and strong. I pulled in every direction against the tension of the stakes and the stiff, stubborn tenacity of the old hardwood. It was taut. I felt proud of my work, my tree. It looked elegant and symmetrical. This was a well planted, monsoon resisting tree that would provide shade and beautify our barren desert campus.

I thanked her for the help and offered to pay for their time. They didn't accept.

"I'm new to the desert and I just didn't know what I didn't know. I was planting kites for the monsoon. I'm going to tell the staff in the morning they have you to thank."

"Mr. Arturo," she replied. "Today I listened to your students. It was hard for me. They are wounded, they are falling, into drugs, some want to die, they don't believe in themselves. I know what is against them. I think you know I didn't stop here to teach you about trees."

18

We worked to stake and support our kids. One of the teachers told me that in Chicago Salesian high school had adopted the slogan, "We may kick your ass, but we will never kick you out." We began to think through how to live that motto.

One place without a stake was juvenile detention. A kid could escape us through that hole in our fence. Our goal was to help raise the next generation, which meant providing the developmental experiences they needed to become positive adults.

How would we do this when they were incarcerated?

Tom Largo had said, "We are adults, and our job is to raise you." But a kid could nullify that intention by getting themselves locked up. After a lot of thinking, we approached the tribe with a radical idea. The jail was just a few hundred yards from the school. We proposed that everything students in the high school received, the students in jail would receive. Our teachers at the jail would offer the same Native Studies and language program. The jailed students would get the same horse therapy, art and beading lessons, compete for prizes when we entered competitions, learn music, and get mentored by Pima elders.

The game changer was football.

We asked the tribal council and police chief if members of the football team could remain on the team even if they were serving time. The council approved with little debate and the police chief set about logistics.

Students in detention were to be driven by police officers to the practice field three times a week. On Fridays, they were to put on uniforms and meet us for pre-game warmups.

Our locker rooms were a stuffy cargo container. The field had been seeded, leveled and was hand-watered by volunteers. Salt River Sand and Rock lent us portable lights that we dragged around the field and hooked up to generators. Our opponents tended to be other small charter schools, mostly the kind for students tossed out of regular schools. The community showed up with folding chairs, and Friday nights became a well-attended and proud event.

Football helped young men ready to sink into self-loathing and criminal identify realize they had a place among "normal kids." They had positive peer pressure, were involved in winning trophies, being heroes in front of their parents, learning to survive criticism and discipline.

For our first Homecoming, we needed better than our hard-scrabble field. We asked for help from a community college that had been built at the corner of the reservation, reminding them they paid one-dollar-a-year to lease tribal land. They resisted, saying our boys would kill their field. After a tough meeting, our final gambit was to threaten that if we could not use their field, then the next day and every day after, their students and faculty would be prohibited from using tribal roads. They could walk to class through the desert. Everyone backed down, and after the success of our Homecoming, the relationship with the college became positive and helpful.

For the Homecoming game, we invited the Sherman Indian Boarding School to be our opponent. They were a storied school with a first-rate all-Indian football team from California. We played in a real stadium for the first time, and the parents from Sherman gave us many thanks: most of them were from the nearby Apache reservation and had never seen their children play in person.

Sherman took it easy on us. They were far superior to our first year, eight-man football team. And we were surprised to find they had girls on the team. The boys at one point said they looked at Sherman's defensive line and realized there were two girls staring them down.

Jesse Tall Elk told me, "I don't know what tribe they're from, but they knocked me over."

We lost but not by much. Mario almost caught the best throw of the game. It bobbled on his fingers as he outran the Sherman defense. We had our first Homecoming queen and a memorable night for all.

Jesse himself had completed his sentence the previous week and had been released from jail. The morning after the game he asked to go back into detention. He told us that there were problems at home and he just wanted to go back to jail, finish school there and have more time to get ready for living on his own.

We met with social service and the tribal judge, and it was decided that for the few months till he turned eighteen, living in jail would be more efficient than finding foster care.

The new African American officer hired to run the detention facility pulled me aside after the meeting to say, "I didn't realize I was here to run a group home, not a jail. Kids playing football and riding horses."

We were standing in the parking lot, staring at Red Mountain, the Pima redoubt during wars. "It's an adjustment, coming from St. Louis. But I'm glad Jesse came back. I'm feeling like they're my kids. When they leave, I want them to make me proud."

19

She was from a reservation where half the kids still spoke Apache, and she had been living with an uncle on the Pima-Maricopa reservation for a semester. She would go home soon.

She had been saving years to collect the expensive eagle feathers needed for a coming-of-age ceremony. This would be an elaborate initiation that took days and involved much of her Apache reservation. It was one of the few coming-of-age ceremonies still intact in the tribal lands.

She had lost one parent to a train and the other to diabetes, but her grandparents took over. Her ceremony was in the planning when, without explanation, her feathers disappeared.

Some in her family argued that it was theft by broke relatives. Her own belief was that spirits took them. It was not her time to be initiated, for reasons only the spirits understood, but it made me very sad.

The story ended well. As word got out, family and tribal leaders put together resources for another set of feathers. To deny a young girl her initiation ceremony was a travesty.

When I asked one of the elders at the Pima senior home about initiation ceremonies, she told me the last she remembered occurred before the river was diverted, and that part of it involved standing on an anthill. Several parents at the school said they were reviving a form of the old Pima initiation for one of the girls.

When I asked about boys, the seniors in the home told me those ceremonies were long forgotten. I asked the same question of my Apache parents in San Carlos, Geronimo's reservation. They said that the male ceremonies had involved skills like hunting, survival and horsemanship. Those skills defined manhood in the old days, but they became obsolete once the tribe was moved to its reservation. The male initiation had disappeared from common memory.

At the school, we asked ourselves what rites-of-passage we could offer, that felt real and signified to young people they were being conferred with adulthood.

Americans often say that they have no culture. That there are no rites-of-passage. But they don't see the water they swim in. There are plenty, and most kids experience them in a sequence that includes first jobs, competitions, licenses to drive and diplomas. Troubled and failing kids, kids with delinquent records, know these initiations by their absence.

Many of our kids had only sporadically attended schools in Mesa, and maybe a third had not attended school at all. They were behind in all areas just as the nation was embarking on the idea that all kids had to march to the same curriculum, at the same pace, and both the school and its students would face consequences for not keeping up. The intentions of No Child Left Behind were noble, but as they have since found, the reasons kids struggle to keep up are complicated.

We had a choice. Graduation is a critical rite-of-passage in Western culture. Everywhere they will ask the date of your graduation and if you have the diploma.

We had kids that read at a third-grade level. They were sixteen. They also needed to learn science, history and mathematics. The dilemma I posed to the staff was straight forward: if we say they can't graduate unless they meet the state standards, most will realize they can't bridge the gap and won't even show up.

And if we say an A in our English class must be the same as an A in the city, then we're setting them up to fail, regardless of effort.

This was hard for staff to confront, but the choice was either stick with the new standards and crush student spirits, or reward character and effort: if a student at sixteen read at the third grade level, but by year's end had advanced to sixth grade, that was a monumental achievement. It had to be rewarded, and not with a D or C, but with an A in tenth-grade English. The student had to experience the rewards of persistent effort.

That's what we did. We took them where they were, taught what was most important, and rewarded them well for making progress. If they mastered essential, basic knowledge, and displayed discipline in their effort, they would walk at graduation. We would be able to say with confidence as they took the diploma, "The tribe welcomes you as an adult, one among us, with faith you will make us stronger."

20

Ray Yazzie started ninth grade as the youngest of several siblings, all of which shared gang affiliation. He had been involved in fights throughout school.

We took him after he was cornered for car theft and the tribal judge said he had to stay on the reservation for schooling. We held a planning meeting, and everyone agreed he should be on the football team. It was coached by a group of dedicated Indian men, one of whom also worked as the school police officer. Mr. Fields, our

Navajo vice-principal, decided to enroll Ray in the school's art program, which he had developed and still co-taught. This would give Mr. Fields a chance to mentor.

Finally, the school counselor placed Ray in our "Academy," a self-contained classroom for students transitioning from incarceration to the high school. There was a strong special education emphasis in the Academy, even if a student didn't have an official IEP. Several aides helped students, and parents were contacted nightly by an assistant who drove to student homes if they did not have a phone.

The first semester, Ray passed courses, did well in football, and received an honor before the community, a first for his family. He was involved in one fight and was sent to a room where unruly students used headphones to engage an interactive lesson about tribal loyalty and expectations. He then spent a period of days in academic seclusion with a stern Indian mentor.

During the second semester, Ray was part of another altercation, and when a teacher tried to break it up, he struck her. Under tribal law, this required incarceration. The police picked him up.

The vice-principal and the teacher he assaulted visited Ray at the juvenile hall. Their purpose was to let him know that while he had earned incarceration, he was nonetheless still part of the school and tribe, and he was not being abandoned. The teacher expressed her continued faith in him, and Ray offered an apology for his actions.

A meeting was held that week with our tribal judge, the chief of police and the director of the detention facility. The school requested that Ray be allowed to practice with the football team once a week and suit-up for Friday nights. The campus police officer who coached would bring him to the game, and afterward return him to the detention facility. All agreed to the plan. Ray's siblings saw a better role-model at the Homecoming game, and his peers on the team continued encouraging responsible behavior.

While in detention, Ray continued to participate in a horse therapy program, art classes, and tutoring with a tribal elder who read one-to-one with him. He had the opportunity to listen to the same invited speakers as visited the secondary school, received Pima language classes, and took part in the brushing and blessing given yearly by the medicine woman. In the spring, the charter school entered a tribal arts competition at the Heard museum, and a solitary, dark figure painted by Ray won a significant prize.

Upon his release, a team assembled to greet him and plan his entry back into the Academy. His parents, teachers and the police were there, as were opposing gang members. The latter were invited in order to get written and verbal understandings that there would be no conflicts when Ray returned to campus. Because several gangs were represented in the Academy, these transitional meetings had to address the issue openly. The meeting was positive, welcoming, and clear as to expectations, standards and hopes.

Ray Yazzie belonged to something bigger than himself, stronger than him and tied to him. It was intent on shaping the boy into a man. The adults were not going to quit and run.

Also by the Author

Shelter

Notes from a Detained Migrant
Children's facility

The Music of Jimmy Ojotriste

A lush, magical tale of street music, love and brujeria

Arturo Hernandez-Sametier
Please visit Lunitabooks.com for more
information on the author.

The Cover Art for this book is from an
original painting by

Esmeralda Piza

Please visit Lunitabooks.com for information
on the artist.